READING POWER

Women Who Shaped History

Grace Hopper
Computer Pioneer

Joanne Mattern

The Rosen Publishing Group's
PowerKids Press™
New York

Published in 2003 by The Rosen Publishing Group, Inc.
29 East 21st Street, New York, NY 10010

First Edition

Book Design: Erica Clendening

Photo Credits: Cover, pp. 9, 13, 14, 17, 18, 19, 20 courtesy Defense Visual Information Center; p. 4 courtesy of Lowell Observatory; pp. 5, 21 © AP/Wide World Photos; pp. 6, 7, 14 Vassar College Libraries, Archives and Special Collections Department; p. 10 © Corbis; p. 11 courtesy of the U.S. Naval Historical Center

Library of Congress Cataloging-in-Publication Data

Mattern, Joanne, 1963–
Grace Hopper : computer pioneer / Joanne Mattern.
    p. cm. — (Women who shaped history)
Summary: A biography of the teacher, inventor, and computer pioneer who worked with the world's first computers.
ISBN 0-8239-6505-8 (library binding)
1. Hopper, Grace Murray—Juvenile literature. 2. Admirals—United States—Biography—Juvenile literature. 3. Computer engineers—United States—Biography—Juvenile literature. 4. United States.
Navy—Biography—Juvenile literature. [1. Hopper, Grace Murray. 2. Computer engineers. 3. Admirals. 4. Women—Biography.] I. Title.
V63.H66 M38 2003
004'.092—dc21

                        2002002929

Contents

In the Beginning

Grace Hopper was a teacher, inventor, and computer pioneer. She worked with the world's first computers. Grace Hopper's work with computers changed the world.

In 1910, when Grace was four years old, her father held her up to look out the kitchen window to see Halley's Comet. Grace liked the comet and her father told her that she would see it again. She saw it again when it came back in 1986.

Grace Murray (Hopper) was born on December 9, 1906, in New York City.

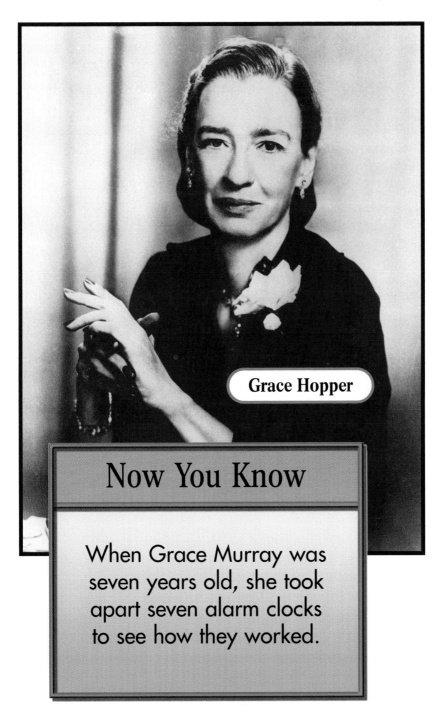

Grace Hopper

Now You Know

When Grace Murray was seven years old, she took apart seven alarm clocks to see how they worked.

Grace's favorite subject in school was math. She earned college degrees in math and physics.

In 1934, Grace Hopper became the first woman to earn a doctorate degree in math from Yale University.

Grace Murray married Vincent Hopper, a teacher, in 1930. In 1931, Grace Hopper got a job teaching math at Vassar College.

Grace Hopper taught at Vassar College for 12 years.

In the Navy

In 1941, the United States entered World War II. Grace Hopper wanted to help her country by joining the U.S. Navy. However, the navy said she was too old and did not weigh enough.

Hopper did not give up. She got special permission from the government to join the navy in 1943.

"A ship in port is safe, but that is not what ships are built for. Sail out to sea and do new things."

—Grace Hopper

Grace had to go to a special school to train for the navy. She graduated first in her class.

Working with Computers

Grace Hopper's first job with the navy was to work on the Mark I computer. The computer was used to help aim naval guns in different kinds of weather.

Grace Hopper received an award from the U.S. Navy for her work on computers during World War II.

First Computer "Bug"

In 1945, the computer Hopper was using stopped working. A moth had gotten inside the computer. Hopper used tweezers to pull the moth out of the computer. She then started using the term *debug* to mean finding and fixing a computer problem. The term is still used today.

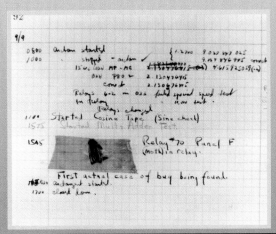

Grace Hopper taped the moth she found inside the computer into her notebook.

"Gee, that's the prettiest gadget I ever saw."
—Grace Hopper's feelings after her first day of work on the Mark I

In 1946, after the war ended, Grace Hopper was forty years old. The age limit in the navy was thirty-eight years old. The U.S. Navy asked Hopper to retire from active duty.

Hopper decided not to go back to teaching. Instead, she went to work for a computer company. Grace Hopper still served in the Naval Reserves after she retired from the navy.

One of Grace Hopper's favorite sayings was "Dare and do."

Hopper had the idea that computers should be able to do more than just math problems. She also thought that computer programs could be written in English.

Grace Hopper's compiler was called the FLOW-MATIC. It was used by businesses. It led to the development of a computer language that would work on any computer.

In 1953, she invented a computer program called a compiler *(kuhm-PY-luhr)* that translates English language instructions into a language the computer understands.

Computer Code

The first computer programs "talked" to computers by using a special number code. This code, or computer language, used only zeros and ones. For example, if you wanted to stop the computer, you would enter "1001100" into the computer's program. It was easy to make mistakes when using this language. It was also very hard to find mistakes once they had been made.

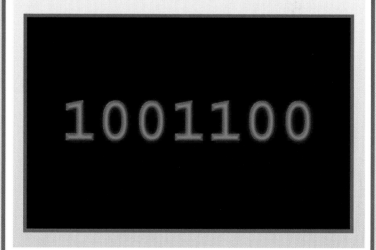

1001100

In 1966, Grace Hopper had to stop working for the Naval Reserves because of her age. People over sixty-two years old cannot be members of the U.S. Navy. However, the navy could not get its computers to work without her. Less than a year after Hopper retired, the navy asked her to come back.

President Ronald Reagan congratulates Grace Hopper for earning the position of commodore in 1983. Two years later, she was made a rear admiral.

After the Navy

Grace Hopper decided to retire from the navy in 1986. She was seventy-nine years old and the oldest officer in the navy. Hopper continued to teach. She also gave speeches all over the world.

Grace Hopper received many awards for her work.

The navy honored Hopper by naming a ship after her. The ship is called the USS *Hopper*.

Grace Hopper said that the day she retired from the navy was the saddest day of her life.

Amazing Grace

Grace Hopper worked with computers until she died on January 1, 1992. She was eighty-five years old.

Her work helped to make computers easier for all people to use. Grace Hopper's ideas made today's computers possible.

Time Line

December 9, 1906
Grace Brewster Murray is born

1930 *Marries Vincent Hopper*

1931—1943 *Teaches math at Vassar College*

1943 *Joins the U.S. Navy*

1945 *First uses the word debug*

1953 *Invents the computer compiler, FLOW-MATIC*

966 *Retires from*
he navy, then is
sked to come back

1986 *Retires*
from the navy

January 1, 1992
Grace Hopper dies

1985 *Becomes*
a rear admiral

1991 *First woman to be*
awarded the National
Medal of Technology

21

Glossary

amazing (uh-**may**-zihng) surprising

commodore (**kah**-muh-dor) a captain in the navy

degree (dih-**gree**) an honor given to someone who has completed his or her studies in a college

doctorate (**dahk**-tuhr-uht) the highest degree given by a college

graduated (**graj**-oo-ayt-uhd) having finished a course of study at a school or college

permission (puhr-**mihsh**-uhn) when someone is allowed to do something

physics (**fihz**-ihks) the study of how matter and power work together

pioneer (py-uh-**nihr**) a person who comes up with ideas that allow for a new way of doing or making things

program (**proh**-gram) an order for a computer that tells it what to do

rear admiral (**rihr ad**-muhr-uhl) an officer with a high position in the United States Navy

retire (rih-**tyr**) to give up working, usually at a certain age

translates (tran-**slayts**) changes from one language to another

tweezers (**twee**-zuhrz) small metal tools that are held between the thumb and forefinger; used for holding and plucking things

Resources

Books

Girls Think of Everything
by Catherine Thimmesh
Houghton Mifflin (2000)

Women Inventors and Their Discoveries
by Ethlie Ann Vare and Greg Ptacek
Oliver Press (1993)

Web Sites

Due to the changing nature of Internet links, PowerKids Press has developed an online list of Web sites related to the subjects of this book. This site is updated regularly. Please use this link to access the list:

http://www.powerkidslinks.com/wsh/grah/

Index

Word Count: 436

Note to Librarians, Teachers, and Parents

If reading is a challenge, Reading Power is a solution! Reading Power is perfect for readers who want high-interest subject matter at an accessible reading level. These fact-filled, photo-illustrated books are designed for readers who want straightforward vocabulary, engaging topics, and a manageable reading experience. With clear picture/text correspondence, leveled Reading Power books put the reader in charge. Now readers have the power to get the information they want and the skills they need in a user-friendly format.